CAPSULE STORIES

Masthead
Natasha Lioe, Founder and Publisher
Carolina VonKampen, Publisher and Editor in Chief
Cover art by Matthew Torres
Book design by Carolina VonKampen

Paperback ISBN: 978-1-953958-00-6
Ebook ISBN: 978-1-953958-01-3

CAPSULE STORIES

Winter 2020 Edition

Published exclusively by Capsule Stories

Contents

Letters from the Editors

It's winter, and we've made it to the end of 2020. I don't think any of us imagined that we would be where we are, doing (or not doing) the things we took for granted, like seeing strangers smile, petting people's dogs, or trying on clothes at the mall. This year has felt like a stripped-down version of reality. Fewer friends, awkward Zoom calls, and feeling invisible as you walk through the grocery store aisles. Loss of life. An indefatigable feeling of loneliness. I hope that there have been moments of joy, and peace, and love, in this year for you. I hope that even though we might all be going through crises, physical, financial, existential, that we remember that the moments in between the chaos are what the point of it all is.
—Natasha Lioe, Founder and Publisher

I've always loved the way bare tree branches look in the winter. I find myself drawn to them as I go for walks in the park or long drives across the countryside. There is such beauty in the patterns they sketch across the gray sky. The trees have nothing to hide behind in winter, and I am in awe of their vulnerability. Being vulnerable isn't easy for me. I'm in awe when writers are able to be so vulnerable on the page, laying bare their grief, sadness, tiredness. This edition of *Capsule Stories* gives writers a place to be open and vulnerable, a sentiment that Glennys Egan captures perfectly in her poem "Being Brave in the Cold": "I'll learn to let / the warm sweater of / my grief fall open / without moving to cover / my bare left breast / . . . / I don't apologize / for what you find." As you read, allow yourself to feel those feelings and be vulnerable. But remember that it gets better, and spring will be here soon.
—Carolina VonKampen, Publisher and Editor in Chief

Content warning: This edition explore themes such as pregnancy/child loss, eating disorders, death, sexual assault, child abuse, and homophobia.

Bare Bones

It begins with the chills in the morning as you pull up the comforter and wish for five more minutes. When you realize that the sky is just a little bit darker, that your windows are fogged up in your car. When you take a walk and look at the massive trees towering over you, branches pointing at the sky, and you wonder, do the trees ever get tired of standing? Perhaps the wind threatens to blow them down, but there they stand, stoic, strong, unmoving. Their colorful leaves have fallen, and their branches are dark, like wooden cracks that have shattered the sky.

Slowly, day by day, the entire world changes.

Being Brave in the Cold

Glennys Egan

Science tells me
and I believe
    why the snow falls
    and the door jamb contracts
    and the plastic cracks
but the liquor doesn't freeze.

How is it, though,
that the trees can stand
        so sparse, exposed
and come spring
still bloom unabashedly
back to life?

Vulnerability
gifted and received;
    their naked dormancy
not punishment
but relief.

Perhaps this is the year
I'll learn to let
    the warm sweater of
    my grief fall open
without moving to cover
    my bare left breast.

The sun low,
your irises expand
    at the sight.

I don't apologize
for what you find.

Come the melt,
when the door begins
to bulge back
against the thresh,
we'll step boldly over it into
a new beginning's light.

*I'll learn to let the warm
sweater of my grief fall open*

Going for Coffee on a Winter's Morning

John Grey

Even in winter,
the dawn is new.

Behind me, rumpled blankets
defy the plain white sheets
of snow drawn up over
hills and fields.
Before the sun
has barely settled
in its rusty chairlift,
all along my path,
I'm leaving deep footprints
in lingering night.

I'm at the wheel
of my car
floating like a hymn
down icy streets,
past fields where
horses move slowly
as if still in their sleep
and the weather snores
deep and gray
behind the clouds.

I walk old rhythms
on the frozen sidewalk,
to where, under the swinging
main street awnings,
men talk of old times,
loudly, excitedly,
like they're just about
to happen.

Winterstorm

E. Samples

This morning there are no shadows or shaded lines
The town is powder caked, entombed
And yet the earth feels overexposed,
Naked in the metal-cold sunshine
January's roughest edges sanded, smoothed
Until familiar streets are alien
I'm a traveler standing on an empty stage
And no map can lead me away from ice

A robin flares between cloaked trees
Its cry a snowball
A squirrel digs a shaved-ice vault
Its feet sugared
A child stomps by a front door
Their boots salted

Wind kicks snow from the brim of my hat
In the cold, in the dawn, in signature solitude
I take off my red glove and submerge my hand
Deep into the beautiful frozen heart of winter

Encounter with Thirty Ravens

Lucy Tyrrell

Originally published in Under a Blushing Sky: Poems about New Beginnings (2020)

The road is trackless with new snow,
a gift in late winter to run on
quilted freshness.
Four dogs lean in harness, pull
my sled over the icy base.

We spin through the recent layer
of white, past bare spots
of gravel and rock, onto the wide
snowmobile trail still
glittering white in the sun.

We encounter no one—
except thirty or so ravens.
They flap and glide,
wheel to skim the pines,
disappear and reappear.

For a moment, in my curiosity
about these coal-feathered souls,
I forget the virus, its contagion,
paroxysms of distance, fear,
fly beyond the unknown path ahead.

The dogs and sled and I course by.
We leave them to their noiseless
squabbles, winged black forms
etching erratic loops and dives
against soft blue and stark white.

Dandelion-Head

Abigail Swoboda

Content warning: sexual assault, child abuse, homophobia

When we let go of the handles of our suitcases and let them fall onto the dust-caked motel bedspread, our fists unfurled for the first time in months. The plume of filth displaced by the suitcases enveloped us like rancid confetti; it concealed from me Jay's grin, but I could feel her smiling. I knew she was smiling because I was smiling. Our happiness was rarely exclusive, though the same could have been said of our sadness, our rage.

"Welcome home?"

"Maybe," Jay said. The dust had cleared, and I could see her face again. "But it's not forever, it's just temporary."

"Most homes are," I said. "But he can't hurt you here."

I left Jay to settle our things in the room so that I could walk around the building—that preternatural urge to gain a sense of one's surroundings.

I hadn't asked Jay if the cigarette smell that was deeply embedded in the fibers of the room bothered her, though I worried. It was better than where we had been, and I could not afford any better. I had saved up for years for this, whatever *this* was. I had worked in a church, then a dog kennel, and then a pit orchestra for *this*. In between shifts I budgeted out room and food for *this*. I liked to tell myself that *this* was freedom, but I could not entirely push from my head the thought that *this* was yet another way of making myself suffer, too. We could stay here for a year with the money I had, but no more.

I walked around the squat motel campus like a jungle cat. Or maybe like an old dog. We had driven close enough so that we could see mountains and far enough so that Jay's dad would not bother chasing after us. The mountains loomed like milky shadows in the distance; Jay's father was much the same. Gravel and leaves crunched beneath my feet in the way they do only on the edge of autumn. The sharp smell of chicken shit and limestone wafted off of the fields beyond the tree line. I felt a wave of embarrassment rush through me; there was something deeply intimate about this smell, something internal, familiar.

And then there was the carcass.

It was a deer, a doe. She didn't look dead. Just like she was sleeping in the broad shadow of the motel. I approached with caution, as if she would suddenly spring up and dart away on her matchstick legs—but she didn't. The body lay with the uncanny stillness of one's face in a darkened mirror. I could not see where she had been wounded; there was no evidence of death besides that unending, disquieting stillness and the smell.

My first instinct was to run and tell Jay, to gather her up in my excitement and bring her back so that we could look at the body together, make an event out of it—but something stopped me. I would not tell Jay about this, could not. I would have liked to think this was altruistic, that I did it to save Jay from one more tragedy, but it was selfish. I did it for me. *This may not have been about me, but this was my body, my one small tragedy.*

I.

The first stage of decomposition is referred to as the *fresh stage*, which begins immediately after the heart stops beating. Blood pools in parts of the body due to gravity, which causes a bluish-purple coloration—*livor mortis*. Within hours, *rigor mortis* sets in and the muscle tissues become rigid, unable to relax.

The body loses its heat to the environment and becomes chilled, cold. Cells begin to lose their structural integrity due to chemical changes in the body's environment in a process known as *autolysis*. This may cause blisters to form on the skin, but overall the physical manifestations of decomposition at this stage are undetectable.

For years, our breakfast had been half cups of coffee and shards of our own fingernails. So that day, when we could not sleep at 4 a.m., I drove us to the nearest diner for enough pancakes and eggs to fill our six-year-long breakfast void. She ordered our food because I had driven because her father had never let her learn how to drive and eye contact made me nervous. We split the bill evenly.

When the waitress left our table we collapsed into giggles. Jay had ordered seven drinks between the two of us (orange juice, apple juice, chocolate milk, Earl Grey tea, Earl Grey tea, black coffee for her, and coffee with cream for me), and the waitress had called her "sweetie" and walked away.

"She's younger than we are, Mary!" Jay said.

We had taken to calling each other by first name more often, as if saying our names made us more real, more present. Jacqueline, Jackie, Jay. Her name had gotten shorter and shorter the longer I knew her, the more urgently I called her to me. The trials and trauma of time had not hardened her as they had so many others. She had not become Jacqueline as Janie often became Jane or Lizzie Elizabeth; she was still Jay as much as she had ever been, Jay like ripping off a Band-Aid. Jay like being stuck at the top of a Ferris wheel. Jay like impatience.

Jay not like "sweetie." Jay was not "sweetie" at all, and never had been. Not even to me.

When our food arrived, we ate with the voracity of crocus on the cusp on spring, gulping down sunlight and praying to photosynthesize, to survive. Our primal desire to consume had long been stifled, and I knew that both of us could hear the disembodied voice of Jay's father echo in our heads: *You're going to get fat. Do you want to end up like your mother? It's a good thing you're young.* Jay's eyes deepened and mine glowed with rage. We kept eating.

By the time we had finished, the diner had filled with hunters sparkling with morning dew. They sat in tight circles, murmuring lowly to one another as they stared with dark eyes into glassy cups of coffee. The striated smears of blood across their jackets matched their cheeks, ruddy from the brazen bite of the early morning breeze.

"It feels like a murder mystery in here." Jay's back was to the hunters. "Who do you think dunnit?"

"We should go soon," I said.

"Where?"

"Anywhere." The word felt sore, like a fresh bruise.

"The light in the closet in our room is dead."

I could not recall noticing the light was out; in fact, I could not remember our ever having tried to turn it on. "So let's fix it."

We paid for our meal in mostly coins, put "White Christmas" on the tabletop jukebox, and melted into the October morning.

I held her hand in the hardware store, felt her hesitation. Her hand was large and warm, unless mine was especially small and cold. Warm hand in cold hand, we walked through the lighting department, where reality was thinner, and imagined a world in which touching never hurt. If fairies existed, they most certainly resided here, among the chandeliers and floor lamps and incandescent bulbs. If happiness existed for us, we knew that it would live here, too, in aisle four, between the hacksaws and the hand drills.

Upon returning to our motel room, I discovered that she was right: the light in the closet was out. In fact, it seemed as though all the lights had burned out. How had I not noticed this before? It was a good thing we had bought a four-pack of lightbulbs.

We went to bed around noon while watching Bear Grylls survive in the Sierra Nevada during a blizzard. I pretended not to hear Jay crying from beside me in the bed. I also pretended that it was the unbiased, spontaneous compulsions of sleep that brought my arms around her. Tenderness was not my mother tongue; it often came to me in broken phrasing, in words mismatched with their intentions. But I was learning.

II.

The second stage of decomposition is the *bloat stage*. Anaerobic metabolism takes place within the body and causes gases such as hydrogen sulfide, carbon dioxide, and methane to accumulate. The accumulation of these gases causes the abdomen to distend and pressure to build inside of the body, causing fluids to excrete from orifices and into the surrounding environment. This pressure may also cause the body to rupture. If insects such as maggots are able to, they

will enter the body and cause skin to slip and
hair to detach from the skin, causing further
ruptures. The odor associated with decay be-
gins in this stage.

The night I cut Jay's hair, we ordered Chinese food for our
Thanksgiving meal and ate it in the bathtub. Our bare knees
bounced in the balmy water beneath our boxes of rice. Tiny,
leftover clipped hairs pricked my skin and made it feel like
tiny bugs were swarming over my hands, my arms, my chest.

"How do I look?" she asked me from across the tub. She
looked at her rice, not at me.

My work was not perfect; her shorn hair stuck out at odd
angles away from her head. What had been my attempt at
intentional style had collapsed into the improvisational, the
makeshift; she looked as if she wore a fuzzy crown of dande-
lion seeds. Jay looked more like herself than she had in years.
Though without a doubt she was, Jay did not look beautiful,
not to me. To me, she looked electric.

"Different," I said.

"Not ugly?"

"No, never ugly."

I could tell she did not fully believe me. She had wanted
to cut her hair for years, but her father had never let her, tell-
ing her that she would look like a boy. He called her a dyke, a
disappointment, worthless. He said she was ugly. He said he
was sorry. But he did not let her cut her hair.

"There is nothing left for him to hold onto now."

"Only wishes now, dandelion-head."

And we laughed instead of talking about the bandages
on her forearms, about the fresh scabs covering my shoulders.

What could we have said? Knowing we were hurting did little to stop our pain. We told ourselves that this pain was part of the process. And we stayed in the bath until the water was cold and our fingers and toes had pruned and become purple and unfamiliar.

III.

The third stage of decomposition is known as *active decay*. In this stage, the most mass is lost due to both the feeding of maggots and the purging of fluids from the body. The purged fluids create what is called a *cadaver decomposition island*, a highly concentrated area of nutrient-rich soil immediately around the cadaver. This may change the chemistry of the soil beneath for years to come. Disintegration becomes evident and strong odor persists. Active decay ends when the maggots depart from the body.

I woke on Christmas morning in a vacant, but not empty, room. And, for the first time since we had been staying there, I woke without fear. I waited for it to hit me, the panic—*Where was I? Where was Jay? What the hell were we doing?*—but, for once, it did not come. Everything was fine. I repeated it several times to try to make it more real. Everything was fine. Everything was fine. Everything was fine. It lost all coherence in repetition, shedding all meaning it might once have had.

Everything was fine. I tried it on like a new pair of shoes. I walked a few steps. *Where was I?* I reflected upon the world we had created over the last couple months. The room was the closest it had ever been to being home for the two of us. For the first few weeks, we had refrained from letting our lives leak into the room. We made the bed; we straightened pillows; we used paper towels as coasters under our water bottles; we left all the extraneous parts of ourselves packed tightly away in the back of my station wagon—we made ourselves easy to love, disappear.

Then one day Jay made microwave mac and cheese for the two of us and I had never seen someone look so beautiful while eating microwave mac and cheese so I drew her eating the microwave mac and cheese and then we both fell in love with her eating the microwave mac and cheese so we went out and bought painter's tape and stuck the picture above our bed. Our bed. We realized that it was not "the" bed anymore, it was *our* bed. So we went back to the store and bought a frame for the picture and nails and a hammer so that we could tack the picture onto the wall because it needed more permanency. The frame was shaped like a set of barn doors. We could close them for as long as we'd like and it would look like a little barn hanging on the wall, then we could open up the doors and there Jay was, eating microwave mac and cheese.

This set off a chain reaction of acts of guerrilla permanency. We stacked our books on the bedside tables, cluttered the TV stand with second grade soccer trophies, switched the white pillowcases out for our mismatched floral ones, let our dirty mugs become an obstacle course on the floor, created a churning sea of clothes on the floor from our communal closet. In our shitty room that smelled like other people's cigarettes, we had cobbled together a home. We knew it wasn't forever, but it was good enough and the doors locked from the inside.

I flexed my toes, then flipped onto my back and held them like a baby in my fists because they were cold. *Where was Jay?* I was still getting used to her independent motion, and so was she. The first few times she left, she had asked my permission out of habit. In the mornings, she had taken to visiting the man who lived in the room three doors down, Mister Bennie, who had three cats. Mister Bennie let Jay feed chicken to the cats and brush the long-haired one, and Jay made tea for Mister Bennie, like she did many nights for me. Jay had wanted a cat ever since she had first met one. Her father had given her a cat four separate times in her life and had subsequently taken it away a week or two later every time. By cat number three, she had learned not to name them. But Mister Bennie's cats were all permanent, even if they were not Jay's, and their names were Scooter, Socks, and Sarah Palin.

Whenever she got back, I would get dressed as Jay told me all about the cats and Mister Bennie and any of the funny things she had thought on her trip but couldn't say to Mister Bennie. It became our morning ritual. After one of the first mornings she had left, Jay asked me if I missed her when she was gone. "Yes," I had said, because I did, "but in a good way. In a way that makes me glad you left so that you can come home and tell me about everything you did while we were apart." I wanted everyone to know Jay, for her to share herself with as many people as possible.

My toes warmed within my fists. *What the hell were we doing?*

Before I could come up with an answer, the door crept open to reveal Jay's shaking silhouette on the threshold. I leaped up. How had it happened again so soon?

"Why did you do it? You didn't have to." She was crying— but smiling.

I relaxed and smiled even wider back. I realized what had happened: She had seen my gift. All around her on the porch, wind chimes sang softly, agitated by the winterbitter breeze. Wind chime after wind chime after wind chime; twelve sets total. Each one of them played different notes; apart they were melodic and lovely, but together they created a terrible, wonderful dissonance.

"I love it!" She rushed toward me, and I caught her in my arms. Hugging was new for us, and we were still kind of bad at it. I never knew where to put my arms, and she never knew how tightly to squeeze. She smelled like coconut shampoo and Mister Bennie's cigarettes. We kept holding on.

"I thought it would be cute, like a twelve days of Christmas type thing, except it's all wind chimes."

"Your present will be finished soon; Mister Bennie just gave me some more yarn!" She broke away from me to show me the contents of the plastic bag she was holding: seven skeins of golden yellow yarn.

Jay had taught herself how to crochet on the internet and had been working on a blanket for several weeks. She said she was making it for me because I was always so cold. She worked quickly; the blanket had grown and grown. It cascaded off the bed now and across the floor. It was a caricature of a blanket, but she insisted that it was not done yet.

So we closed the door and sat on the floor because that was always the best place to sit. Jay began to crochet the golden yellow yarn into the blanket, which was already four other colors, and I began to draw her crocheting as the faint ring of discordant wind chimes provided for us a distant score.

I tucked my toes beneath the blanket and felt them grow warm.

IV.

When active decay ends, *advanced decay* begins. Decomposition slows because of reduced insect activity. When on soil, the vegetation around the carcass will die, but the cadaver decomposition island will display an increase in soil carbons and nutrients, promoting future growth in the area.

The winter was brutal that year, but survivable. In mid-February, the whole motel lost power for two days. Jay and I worked quickly and efficiently; within an hour, the oil lamp was lit, there was a pyramid of canned food, all door and window frames had been blocked to prevent drafts, and an impressive blanket fort took up most of the room.

On the first day of the outage, Jay and I shared jokes, read poetry aloud, and told each other secrets that we were too afraid to tell under the fluorescent spotlight of artificial lighting.

On the second day of the outage, Mister Bennie joined us with his three cats in tow. "We are stronger in numbers," he had said. So the three of us sat on the floor together and shared the warmth of the oceanic expanse of the blanket Jay had made for me, which could have covered the space of the entire room then. We played Pictionary, then Clue, then UNO. I won our final game of UNO, and Mister Bennie asked if he could hug me. I said no and he smiled, understanding, and we shared a high-five.

Night approached and our games ended. Mister Bennie told us stories from his childhood, and Jay and I allowed ourselves to get lost in his world for a while. When we cried, Mister Bennie held our hands gently and told us not to be sad because his life was not a tragedy.

"It can't be too bad if it led me here with you two," he said, and it only made us cry harder because he was so sweet and because the world was so fucking absurd.

While fingers of harsh winter light still slipped in through the window, Mister Bennie took out a dry erase marker from his impossibly large handbag. I hadn't seen one of those markers since graduation a few years back. I reveled in the vulnerable sensation of nostalgia it gave me. He emerged from under the cover of the blanket, and I noticed for the first time how small his legs were. Wordlessly, he walked to the window and wrote in all caps TOM. We nodded, understood. Jay got up and took the marker from Mister Bennie. DAD, she wrote, paused, erased it with the back of her hand, then wrote his full name, which I realized I had never actually known before.

There was an empty moment between any action while we looked at their names side by side, thought about what they had meant to us in the past, wondered what they would mean to us in the future. It seemed too simple to be able to write them out this way, to just make several marks on a window and have them suddenly standing there in front of us.

Then the moment ended and I got up too and, together, the three of us wrote down all the nasty things we had been called in the past—all the words that had been thrown at us in the past, all the phrases. Those things that we had kept stashed in the furthest penumbrae of our brains, we wrote them on the window, boldly, in capital letters, for everyone to see.

We stopped when the whole window had been covered, almost entirely blackened with insults, cruelty. They seemed

---

ridiculous all together like that, satirical, but we knew that we had once believed them all. The waning winter sun shone in through the window and cast the words across the room: across the floral pillowcases, across the soccer trophies, across the sea of blanket, across Mister Bennie, across Jay, and across me, too.

We sat back down on the floor and allowed the words to touch us, to crawl across our chests, suckle on our marred flesh. We acknowledged the pain they had caused us and let ourselves feel that pain now again, fully, without resistance. It was a familiar pain, but it carried different meaning than it had in the past; the pain was not less, but transformed. We let it touch us and dared, finally, to touch it back. We shook hands and exchanged names. *Hello*, we said. *Hello*, it said back.

As time passed, the light changed, and we watched the words stretch and warp until they were so distorted that they were unrecognizable, meaningless.

"Did you know he used to touch me?" Jay said flatly.

She had never talked directly about what her father had done to her before. "Yes," I said.

We realized that there was nothing we had to talk about.

"But he never will again," Mister Bennie said as if ending a prayer.

The light of day faded away, and we were released from the words' fetters. Against the blackness of night, we could no longer see the words printed on the window, but they were still there, though we no longer bore their marks on our skin.

We all slept on the floor, huddling together for warmth like penguins. When she fell asleep, Jay did not convulse with tears as she so often did in the throes of stark nighttime, and so Sarah Palin fell asleep on Jay's chest over the smooth, rhythmic waves of her gentle breathing.

V.

The final stage of decomposition is the *dry* or *remains stage.* In this stage, all that remains of the cadaver is dry skin, cartilage, and bones. When all soft tissue is removed, the cadaver is referred to as completely *skeletonized.* Infused with nutrients from the decomposed body, the area around the cadaver will experience a resurgence of plant life. The effects of the decomposed body will manifest in its surroundings for years to come.

Jay and I left the motel in late April. Our hearts flickered like lighter flames, as if we could keep our light dancing for as long as we could keep our thumbs pressed down on the button. We shivered from the cold, the sweetness of the air. We packed our tiny life back into our station wagon and practiced looking forward. My wind chimes had been blown away in one of the many winter storms, and we said goodbye to them without malice. Jay's blanket was too large to fit into the car, so we left it in the room for someone else to find their warmth in.

I had taken one final lap around the motel early that morning, early enough that Jay was still asleep like the rest of the world. The doe was still there, but now she was only bones. I had not seen her body disappear, but it was gone nonetheless. The one goodbye I had to say was to her, and when I said it I gave her back my borrowed tragedy. She was free, I thought, but she had been for a while already.

Later, I wrote a note to whoever would stay there after us, be it only for a night or for a lifetime, and slipped the piece of paper like a bookmark between the pages of the Bible in the bedside table.

Having said her goodbyes to Mister Bennie and Scooter and Socks and Sarah Palin, Jay was already in the car when I hopped into the passenger's seat. She had just gotten her license the week prior. When I entered the car, it was like stepping into a new plane of reality. Here, the pedals no longer lay beneath my feet.

"Are you sure you can do this?" I asked Jay.

"Yeah, yeah, definitely," she said, "but before we go … look!" She held her hands out in front of my face, fingers splayed and wiggling. Her fingernails looked normal, which they hadn't ever since I had known her. She had, for years and years, bitten them far down the nailbed so that they were only stubs, but now they extended past her fingers; they were longer than mine. I could see the translucent line under the enamel where she had bitten them down to over and over again.

In response, I took off my sweater and showed her my shoulders revealed by the tank top I wore beneath. I had not worn a tank top since the seventh grade. My shoulders had not seen the sunshine for so long—it felt impossibly warm. "I haven't been picking at them as badly anymore. I'm not as afraid of people seeing my scars."

We could both feel it: we were healing. But we could also both feel the urge to destruct, to make ourselves suffer again as we had for so many years. Growth was a beast of duality.

"Let's stop and get some nail polish," I suggested.

"Only if it's red." She lowered her hands and curled her claws around the steering wheel.

"Candy apple, cherry, scarlet, garnet, blood—any red you want."

And so we left.

Ask Me What It Was Like to Be Raised by an Angel and a Devil

Eva Lynch-Comer

Mami sent me songs
on the backs of dragonflies.
Father rocked me in a cradle of thorns.

Mami wore a halo of pine cones,
rushed to save me, but it was no use
for I could not even save myself.

I pulled my braids until
they thinned like yawning grass,
I ate until my thighs were fat,
curved my shoulders, stomped
my feet until they grew holes
in their soles, memorized
the smell of graphite on paper.
But I could not keep
his fingerprints from my skin.

Every time I breathe
my chest stings.
I do not know
who to hate more.

Once Mami has wiped
the tears from my eyes,
I have wiped the tears
from hers, we find
the thorns and needles
that lie in the open spaces

of my heart. I pull one out,
she pulls one out.
We cover the thorns
and needles we have picked
in a warm silk cloth, place them
on the backs of dragonflies.

Together, we sing a song to each wound.

*We sing a song
to each wound.*

In Morning

Eva Lynch-Comer

I wake up early
give myself permission to
start this day though the

shame still stings. I dab
lavender oil on
my wrists, inhale so

deep it burns my nose.
The oil is like a rubbing
alcohol. It heals

from the outside in.
I put on my rings. Silver
wheat ring so I can

remember to be
patient as I wilt and grow,
wilt, grow, wilt, grow, wilt . . .

Ring of hearts shaped like
infinity signs circle
the left ring finger.

No one is here to
sniff the fragrance or admire
the heart and wheat rings.

My dad left me first.
So, I lash out at my friends
or hold them too close.

This way, they cannot
leave me without warning. I
decide when they go.

I have pushed away
three close friends in three quick months.
Success shouldn't taste

this bitter. During
my last session with my old
therapist, I asked

her for a list of
other counselors in the
area. I dig

up the paper from
the bottom of my purse, smooth
the wrinkles, dial

three different numbers,
one per friend I pushed away.
Make an appointment.

Before bed, I place
rose quartz above my pillow
hope love will seep in.

hope love will seep in

Unkissable

Swastika Jajoo

---

it is winter and i am still convinced
of the undesirability of my body.
the season for self-love is always
the next one and the plea to a lover constant:
please love me but please do not insist
on seeing me. with the lights switched off,
at least the loneliness is not so bright
that it hurts your bones, at least
you can pretend that you still
have something to give.

for many queer bodies,
most of the tiredness of desire
comes from its disallowance.
there is not enough love,
and no love is enough.

It's Winter and I Fall in Love

Eddie L House

It's snowing and there are cotton wool puffs caught up in our hair, shining bright against the midnight blue dye I used last night. We duck and giggle under bare branches as they catch and tangle, stomp ice shards beneath our boots. The days come and go this winter, like rain showers in April. We baptize ourselves as flakes fall, stroke them from each other's shoulders.

How I wish we had been fearless. How I wish we had been careless enough at fifteen to strike lightning where we stood. To reach out, cradle that pink-red storm cold lobe of your ear. To taste your chapped lips. We could have been intimate; we could have been infinite.

We tackle, roll snowballs, dive away then return. Our bodies synchronize, like dancing, but rowdier. The streets are silent bar our laughing screams. The windows of houses cast us in a glow.

It's a cold and long winter this year, but it won't be a lonely one. We dip into the comfort of one another and know

spring will warm our bones soon.

slain spring

Linda M. Crate

what was meant
to be happiness and joy
a birdsong that saved me
from an endless winter,
you were instead
the flower that died in a
cruel laugh of winter;

leaving me suspended
in these bleak and barren bones
chilled to the core—

born in summer
i have never much cared for
the cold

or the death of flowers,

and i never got to hold your hand
or hear your voice or hold you;

and when i see mothers with their
living children sometimes i am jealous
of all the chances i missed out on—

maybe your father and i were never meant to be,
but i would rather not have lost you.

ebbing

Shufei Ewe

the early december wind by the harborside is fraught with a bitter bone-chill that nips at your ankles. the restaurant lights pulse against the river surface, languidly teasing the pocket of your heart you've hollowed out ———— a space for the slow tango between anticipation and bitter disappointment. you count the number of times you could've left in bated breaths, bathed in the afterglow of the 4 p.m. sunset. you wonder why the sun caressing the skyline makes you wonder how this is worth it when *this* has no name. the walk back home is shadowed by the slivers of the evening sky in your wake. you gaze briefly at the stars that dangle out of reach, with an illuminating pang of envy, then withdraw inside and double lock your door. in the dim obscurity of your room you finally shrug off the weight of existing with a cocktail of duvet covers, leftovers, and half-sleeps to forget a face that flickers into your dreams. you keep the hallway light on so you can watch love leave, in a whisper, while you wait for something that will never arrive.

Haikus for My Daughter

Morgan Russell

I carried the moon
in my shirt, begged her to stay.
Nine months in, she left.

Oh, she stayed with me
for a bit. She comes and goes.
Pulls me in at low tide.

She leaves with the stars,
my thumbprint in the night sky.
I'd call her home if—

I thought she'd stay,
but I carried her to ebb
out to light my sky.

Monsoon of Mediocrity

Morgan Russell

I'm
stuck. a
constellation
uttering wickedly

Help;
i gilded
the lily but
i'm lost inside

Loss
echoes
mania, which is
to say mostly melliferous

Chaotic bells
chime at night
twice now i've
called: hark! she's near you now

At night
i am what?
the i that is me is lost
inside it too.

I Guess This Is Goodbye

Savannah Cooper

---

*You have shrunk my world
to the space between two fingers
and expanded it beyond galaxies.
I didn't know it was possible to feel
at once small and infinite, larger
than the sky and calmer than the height
of spring.*

That's what I would have said if ever
we'd met, if ever you grasped my finger
with your whole hand. I wrote those words
a month ago, anticipating seeing your face,
imagining 3 a.m. with you and the dim light
through the back window. I was ready to be
a poet again for you, to be anything
your racing heart required of me.

I don't know if there are words beyond these—
or worlds, for that matter. I don't know if
we'll ever meet again on some far-off golden shore.
All I know is these days have to be enough,
these moments of seeing you in every room
of every place I've been, your hand in mine,
your voice a song I'll never get to learn.

My head is full of plans to fill the quiet,
to populate this void with daisies, but all this
could never erase you. These streets were meant
for you, not me, and if I laugh extra hard or drink
a little too much or stand listening to the rain
fall through the trees, know that I am thinking of you,
of the way you waved through the dark.

Elegy

Savannah Cooper

Death came to her slowly, his fingers
ticking along her skin, leaving behind
little red marks of disease and doubt.
She paled with each phase of the waning
moon, grayed with every fraught sigh.
She coughed and diminished.
Phone calls became impossible,
text messages obsolete. Her eyes retreated
into her skull, her mind into a cave.
An unused ashtray rested on the mantle,
wildflowers on the windowsill. Their color
faded before touching her sunken cheeks.

I buried her late on a Wednesday night.
There was snow on the ground. The shovel
blistered my hands. I tried to sing a lullaby,
a lament, but on every note,
my voice cracked.

No one visited the unmarked grave,
the little hill of dirt and mud, black
in the snow, brown come spring.
No fingers brushed that earth but mine,
and eventually not even I walked
that ground. She slept alone,
and I did not dream of her.

Loose Strings

Savannah Cooper

Everything feels like a metaphor these days.
The binding of the book on my nightstand
is coming undone—frail, hair-like strings,
almost invisible, slipping loose. I pull on one
until it snaps and hangs past the spine, ruptured,
a thread to worry. Too heavy-handed
if I made it up, but reality isn't subtle sometimes.
There's no artistry to it, just blunt imagery.
Blank walls and found photos and the way
all the pale pink flowers have been beaten
off the tree in the backyard.

It's only symbolism because my mind
can think of nothing else, turning
the same thoughts over and over
until I have to reroute them, have to snap
the lights off each time they flick on
in that room. The door has no lock,
but I can turn away each time my feet
drag me to the threshold. I can avert my gaze.
I can sigh and go in, but only so often,
returning with red-rimmed eyes
and a paler face, feeling like tissue paper.
One good rainfall, and I'm in pieces.

One Day

Savannah Cooper

A scrap of paper fluttered, lost,
caught like a leaf in a twisting wind.
She reached out to grasp it, her fingers
pinching the air, closing on the strangled blue
of the November sky. Smirked, said nothing.

I almost told her the thing I'd dreamed
and understood, dreaming, the stark truth of—
one of us will bury the other someday, unless
we both go down in sudden fire, hand
clasping hand, screaming or laughing or flinging
our fragile bodies off a lonely cliff.

One day, I'll have to say goodbye to you.
The words heavy as paste on my tongue.
She stood in the grass across the road, reaching
for a red feather stuck to a tree. Looked up,
touched my eyes with hers, grinned.

Fantoccini

Kirsten Luckins

The clouds today are the blue-black of eye bags.
The trees blaze against them, rebels to a sapling.
Pointillist berries transport the green shadows with scarlet.
The haws are set, thumb-prick carmine,
and the sloes are blue as ravens.

Along the old embankment, crowds of rosebay
have withered to a froth of seed-split pods
swaying on rattles of madder leaves.

The gray wind.

Long-vacated, you melt
into the arms of the earth,
sockets deep as inkwells.

In twelve years, the scientists say,
the damage will be irreversible.
Your son's lifespan, again.

A break in the clouds reveals the trees
are full of shadow-puppets. They tell folktales
about the beginnings and ends of worlds.

One Way

Natalie Marino

The nights are dry again,
nights of autumn in Los Angeles
are more wind than cold,
one way we know it is not spring.

In this city without seasons,
our hair turns gray,
the only thing around here
to remind us of snow.

We replaced the dark green garden
with bright pink desert flowers
reflecting the light of the moon.
Another way we know.

In spring, time is never-ending.
When we think about the edge of earth,
we are silent in our fear,
and then sad.

Now that we are covered in ash,
joy is quiet too.
We still remember grabbing
the first orange daffodils.

Last Photograph

Natalie Marino

My grandparents stand
close to each other
smiling at the camera

in faded blue raincoats.
My grandfather's hat
curls at the edges.

They are thin
string beans,
still saving space.

Americans who
never grew out
of immigrant clothes,

they could not stop
collecting
cherries in jars.

A white awning
above them
is bright as blank paper,

and it reminds me this house
was identical to twenty
neighbors' houses, new in 1953.

The tired gray
clouds above them
will not last long.

Backbone in Minnesota, Winter

Nancy K. Dobson

For Marie

Marie looked at her daughters the morning after Harry died,
sleep in their eyes, milk on their chins,
sold her pearl brooch, then paid the undertaker,
but she refused to part with the sable.
There was money for a small marker with Harry's name and dates,
but not quite enough to engrave a cross.
Marie doubted Harry would mind;
he never asked for a priest, not even at the end.
Collecting Harry's life insurance, the sum of which fit
in the silk lining of her alligator purse, more decisions were made.
Marie bobbed the girls' hair, let down their hems,
sold the silver tea service and all twelve sets of bone china.
But first, before packing it in the newspaper-lined crate,
she cupped a gold-rimmed teacup in her palm
and tried to remember the last words she spoke to her husband.
She studied her hands before slipping on her gloves,
her strong and direct fingers,
so distinct from her small frame and shy voice,
uneasy when she slid them in the sable's slim pockets.
She envied Harry, every obligation forgiven now,
but for Marie there was a basket of mending to tend to
and an emerald ring to pawn at the Bank Street jeweler.

No Socks for a Martyr

Nancy K. Dobson

My eyes blur at your four-line letter
crumpled like dirty jeans.
I should turn on the lamp, so my eyes
don't strain but then I might write a reply
with hands that ache to betray me.
Some days I slouch in my big shirt,
and ignore small comforts
that could be mine, a quick flip
of the pillow to feel the cool side on my cheek.
I sniff out your presence in old shirts,
or look through books you forgot,
sterile pages of history, but one grainy photo stops me,
a woman who followed a man west in 1886,
streaks of gray in her hair but another baby
on the way. Her face is lined with stubbornness.
It will be a hard winter; the children need shoes,
but she pulls a rickety plow, plucks a scrawny chicken,
frowns and finds a way while here I am,
bare feet on frosty floorboards,
refusing to turn up the heat even as my skin cracks,
I congratulate myself on my hard-earned pain
and wait for it to make me strong.

Thrill Seeker

Nancy K. Dobson

Yesterday, I guzzled two glasses of the tap water
you warned me about, and climbed the tree
you said could not hold me,
its branches rigid with ice.
Last night I let you hold me long enough
to place a kiss on each link of my spine,
melting me down to my purest, most essential form,
the one willing to surrender.
I speed to morning yoga where my spine
is a chain I lift to the sky,
every muscle—back, legs, arms—grips the mat
to fight, or maybe obey, each command
called from the front of the room
where scented candles sigh. I yield
to the floor with the next exhale.
We finish by breathing in thirds, the key
is to not let each gust out too fast.
I drive home, keep my car under the posted limit,
but I would love a little rain right now
to speed up under fat drops, a shout of thunder,
enough slick on the road
that I grip the wheel tighter
and it feels a little bit dangerous.

black ice/ haiku

Isabella J Mansfield

---

black ice on asphalt
undetected, unseen. The
lie is the danger

Some Years Are Like That

Isabella J Mansfield

some years
it snows early
for a long time
and everything becomes
padded, silenced
I swear in those moments
          if you stand still long enough
you can feel the Earth slow down
just a little, feel the whirring
of snowfall around your cheeks
some years though—
some years the ice is so thick
it loses its transparency
the air steals the breath
from your lungs
and redistributes it

Body
of Water

Isabella J Mansfield

---

when winter sets in,
the lake loses
energy to the
atmosphere—
it will
first freeze
around
the edges
before ice
takes it
completely

somewhere / places

Noah Letscher

Somewhere
there is a lake on this campus

I do not know
if it is
placid
or if winds whip its wintery waters
or if ice crackles under the bright stars of Orion

what I do know is that

first year's roommate thought to
dip themselves dying beneath its surface
but found it frozen

Frost, twined its surface
space, black, nebulaeic
cream swirling in coffee
or so I'd imagine, but it was somehow warmer then than it is now
unless I am remembering things wrong

Things lose themselves in my mind
dip themselves deep till I cannot find them
search though I may through the
forest, frosty, spikes
of my heavy mind
of my heavy
crown

---

too full of remembering
too empty of letting go
dip
dying
frost-laced thoughts
placid waters
carrying belts and crowns
of constellations

wind ruffles waters and then
they lie
still

too full of remembering
too empty of letting go

Stranger

Nick Newman

I don't know the person in the mirror.
I look in the glass and instead of the thin, nervous face I know,
someone serious stares back
and no matter how much

he grimaces and winks and grins, moustache
twitching like a zapped rat,
the smile never reaches his eyes and they are never my eyes.
I chart a map. I squirm down
the brainstem, rattle the ribs of his cage, sail
the tributaries of his veins but
       they are not mine. I am not his.

I caress the patchwork nerves, feel them pulse,
observe a chemical signal that passes
across the synaptic gap, sparking neuron
after neuron until fingers spasm,
convulse, reach out for the man who told them to move,
but they close on absence.

I am not here.
I stand apart from the white-knuckled creaking frame,
gaze skittering

hanging
    weightless,
        waiting for the moment
           this body feels like home again.

the season that preys

john compton

cold froze
the veins in my house.

it sits, skeleton
bare to the elements.

i lie inside its battered skin
digested by the chill.

weather knocks on its eyes
waiting to come in, wanting

to feel the heat
from its heart pumping

murmurs
trying to keep up.

x

my feet burn
in the fourteen-degree air.

i exchange promises
to keep from hypothermia.

even in my blankets
i feel i am not safe

from the black discoloration
of dying flesh.

i wear you

john compton

---

like a blood clot.

i fear you will move
too swiftly
and take out my heart.

i kiss the aspirin taste
from your lips.
every day we get thinner.

now we wait.
i clean up
with a glass of milk

and eat
our only truths.

Asking the Proper Questions

Mallory Pearson

If I couldn't eat then, how could I do it now?

Pushing around tomatoes,
tossing them over my shoulder,

reaching blindly for the dog
 under the table.

What's that animal innocence like?

January came and still I was
debilitated by the idea of sleeping on my back.

If you asked me now I'd say
for me, that winter was like ricocheting

off the back of a bird, my arms outstretched,
my body this heavy thing with the memory of being hit.

Even if it mattered,
I wouldn't touch it.

I've been waiting on this bridge
for what feels like something endless.

Good Night Call

Swastika Jajoo

---

when i tell my aunt, "it must be difficult to be alone in these
times" she laughs,
adjusting the phone screen slightly
so her face shifts from fuzzy to distinct,
just like the loneliness she will tell me of:
"you know, i have been alone for a decade now.
how does it matter?"

she tells me she can't sleep
and i tell her i cannot either.
the sound of my bones is too loud
and i always want to stay awake to make sure
the sun rises.
my aunt tells me she has been praying, and i
ask her if she has eaten breakfast. she says
no, and i wish i could tell her eating and hydration
are forms of prayer, too, aunt, the altar is you
and there is nothing as holy as buttered toast.

instead, i just say "please eat,
will you?" she says
"yes, i will" before disconnecting but i know
that she will not, because i know
that i will not either
but both of us will still say we will.

We Are a Family of Snow People

Swastika Jajoo

i am trying to learn by heart
how my fourteen-year-old brother falls asleep on my mother's
lap and touch itself is a lullaby—
there are times when the four of us
are this close to a hug but we don't hug.
even holding your hands out to the people
you love very much is an act of courage.
i don't expect the frost on my tongue to melt
each time i say the word *family*
because maybe the frost is the reason we stay.

my mother has a bias for blue clothing
so when i see this sadness wrap itself around her
i think that it is also blue.
as it wraps itself around her,
with each turn she falls for it
over and over again.

when my little brother tells me that feelings are stupid and
existence, meaningless,
i half want to punch him for his cynicism
but i don't because we both know where he got it from.
when my father says i love you is a ridiculous thing to say
i want to say waves of i love yous to him
so we are facing the river like we have been all this time but
now we are holding hands.
there are many ridiculous things left to be said.

i keep thinking we're on a skating rink
and none of us know how to skate
but even the sound of unsure wheels against the ice floor can
spell love,
that we're all making fools of ourselves
all bundled up and the tips of our noses frozen
but we're falling for and on each other
and we have no option but to hold on and hold tight
because we are all we got
and we'll dance and drop to whatever music they play.

hold on
and hold tight

A Flower behind My Grandfather's Ear

Swastika Jajoo

my grandfather has returned
and he wears striped blue today, his sleeve
an extension of the winter sky. he does not know it is winter,
his arms heavy with seasons
that always promise to come but never stay.
his speech is muffled spring. i struggle
to understand when he calls out to me
but i know there is a flower somewhere.

today, the sun is out and so we sit
together in the lawn. he thumbs his left wrist,
where is my watch, he asks.
what time is it, he does not ask. *what day is it*,
he does not ask. *who are you*, he asks.
where is my watch and *who are you*.
i reply with a rare hug. i do not want
to confuse him with more names.

i bring him a flower whose name i don't know
and he wears it behind his ear, his skin either
a glint of gold in the warm sunlight or
a burning sore. he sips on his tea
and hums to the only song i have heard him hum to.
when he is tired
he asks to be taken inside.

i follow him in, my poem settling
in his sky-sleeve, becoming both keeper and kept of a grief
that will not be put into words; it reads:
A Flower Behind My Grandfather's Ear
and other beautiful things that bleed.

Early Onset Freeze

Mary Alice Dixon

Tongues cast in ice
freeze my memory's dress
unstitching
once plump cloth

dispensing
to the custody of others
the threads
of my good graces,
if such there ever were,
of who I used to be
when I wore myself as me
before this winter's
early advent.

What self is left to pray
for my remaining me,
my fabric ragged
under drift of snow.
Even my name is buried.

There Will Be Too Much to Restore

Kayla King

---

for Notre Dame

Now the memory isn't quite clear.
Feel ancient, perhaps, for photos
are filtered to look that way. But thinking
back remains a corrosive plight.

There are the streets, of course,
the Opera House, that building on the hill.
You turned eighteen that year.

But here is the feeling of forgetting;
fragmentary. People are nothing
more than empty cathedrals waiting
for worship.

Focus now on the sanctity of that,
which you tell when too drunk.
Back then, you found the answer
in a text.

Even now, words remain
religion. But do you not cling
to others? To recollections?

You're possessive over those
postcards, paper skin marred by the details
you couldn't relinquish.

Is it true? Did this happen?
But that version of you is not here
to ask and panes of glass look familiar

only in other people's photos.
If you know anything at all,
recall this as temporary,

something to harness against the plight
in a poet's mind. But the camera is missing,
and there is no evidence to trace beneath finger,
no way to emerge from the engulfing exhalation

across the world.
Breaths held, tragedies forgotten,
but for the spire crashed

down to the floor. And you cannot claim it
as a sign of anything but the passage
of time.

do you not cling

to others?
to recollections?

Like Water in the Palm of My Hand

Lois Roma-Deeley

It hurts to look
at the medieval cathedral sitting high on a hill
and then walk through the rough doors
only to discover the delicate fresco inside its dome
darkened so by centuries of candle smoke and prayers.

Gray-faced angels poke their wings through dingy clouds,
pointing at the heads of shipwrecked sailors
bobbing in a grimy sea of loss.
But why am I surprised at the vivid reflections

on the mosaic stone floor, swirling around both feet;
how the rosettes of muted greens, cobalt blues, wine reds
could be an obvious answer
to the only question my heart is afraid to ask?

Courage is needed to look up again
into the vaulted ceiling, which pushes and pushes skyward,
while wondering how those stone arches could carry the weight
of so much of my own longing.

Suddenly, the tapestry hanging on the back wall billows
like a friendly wave from another life,
the one I could have lived. Now I begin to see
into the design this scene
where a terrified doe jumps into the forest of Ash
while three hounds nip at an archer's heel.

And now, like water in the palm of my hand,
I'm dropping through time,
understanding more than I can know. . . .

But the eternal now quickly slips away
leaving me alone in this shallow winter light.
And I can't explain how I came here
or why this ancient weaving deeply wounds me.

Perhaps it was the wind—
or something like the wind—
coming through an open window,
which released an arrow from the archer's bow
piercing my heart like this and just so.

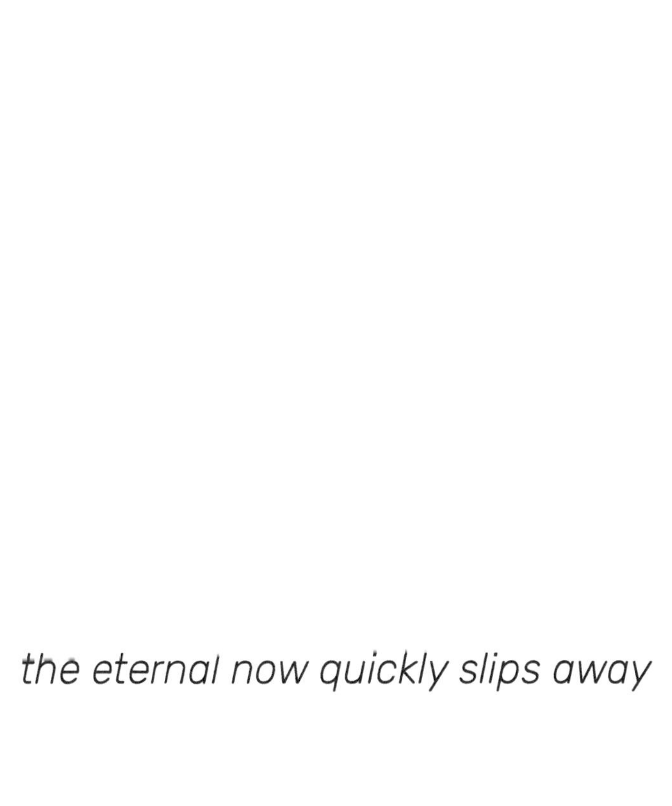

the eternal now quickly slips away

Bone Memory

Kayla King

Yes, but hear me out:
you were ruthless in your pursuit
to ruin, and she's here
for your artistry.

Maybe it was worth the brokenness
to let light lick through fissures
in your exterior. Fragility of half-ghosts
ribboned with gold fuse you back
in a romantic way. And she said you were more
beautiful for having been shattered
so long ago.

But you must remember the time you broke
your ankle, the way it still cracks in the middle
of the night when you walk
in your sleep.

Do you dare
disturb her? She is not the universe,
but she is created out of you. Feel her
in your bones; this is where you miss her
most. Ache at the thought of feeding
her marrow from your wishbone.

There is also your backbone, which you found
too late. You'd already been splintered
by your own silence, missing spine
slicing you thin. But you were put
back together again in a herringbone pattern

by the promise of a prophet
with cards in the pocket
instead of the cigarettes you hated.
Not for the smell, but the taste of words
after smoking.

And there were others:

Fish bones plucked from teeth
on a first date where you denounced a belief
in motherhood, because you couldn't
imagine giving all of yourself
to someone.

Recall the ravine of ribcage,
picked apart by scavengers on the side of the road.
You only looked for the heart, because
the soul is nothing but bone
we don't bother.

you couldn't imagine giving
all of yourself to someone.

Farewell Is a Thing without Feathers

Kayla King

Think there were a handful of months
where hunger cleared our minds. We bathed
in ink to walk with shadows, to disappear
into the seam of the Seine where water dares
not disturb the voyage
of lovers.

You stayed,

and I left.

Such was a talent bestowed,
the temporary contempt for reckless
reciprocity with my mother. She, too, slipped
off into darkness while I slept. And did she wish
things for me, as I do you? Perpetual fog, Post-it note
promises for better days, plates that never empty;
I wish you many things.

I must incant on the back of the postcard before
burying these words. I can't have them
close, will not let them dissuade
from my distance.

There is hardship in heartstrings, and I won't let you
unloose mine now. Instead, I rip the binding
from your favorite book, press this penance inside.

I carve out a hollow of earth
with my fingers. If you were here
you'd press your face to my hand, breathe in
the scent of mulch, too much like your mother's garden.
Hydrangeas in bloom, trickle of water, pennies
for a better blue; these were all a wish for settling.
But I always sidestepped talk of side
by side for something more,
unmooring myself time and again

for this moment. Now you're missing
from me. You flip coins over on street
corners, wishing luck to strangers,
but always seeing me in their faces.
It's something we have
in common, this

Hope.

There is more to be had, for sure:
fragile tart shells meant for filling, teacups
overcrowded with cherries, a pitcher of cucumbers
and gin; feed the space I've left behind.

You stayed,

and I left.

A Memory of Winter, Denver

Barbara Simmons

Later, I would describe our time as colorless,
winter had taken care of that, whiteness over all,
your apartment gleamed modern, silver, Scandi,
tubular arrangements holding all you owned
together. A few times we tried the trails around
the campus where you taught, our herringboned
tracks revealing how unsteady we were.
Later, driving to the airport, winter
pelting us with sleet, the wipers froze,
clock hands to the hour two, mocking us, our
mittened cleaning of the windshield
only cleared one side.
A colorless goodbye, the blandest promises
to stay in touch, a mutual relief in boarding, leaving.
Far below, a winter without powder had gone
straight to ice.

The Cell Phone Rings inside My Pocket

Lois Roma-Deeley

I won't answer.
I never do.
Instead, I place the heartleaf philodendron
on the kitchen windowsill
as if the rising winter sun has come
to celebrate this moment of possibility.
Tomorrow I'll clean the backyard
stripping the willow bark of dead leaves
piling them onto a cord of split wood
and a grate of concrete.
Snow will fall onto my wild hair.
How should I think of love now?
My fingers, numb from cold,
fumble for a match.
Then I blink, twice. The snow will fall
suddenly and without warning,
pushed by a fierce wind,
it drops against the back door
like a fighter slumped in a corner
after going down for the last count.
Picnic benches, fence posts,
even the ceramic gnome you set in the garden,
will be covered
with the singleness of cold, the push of winter.
I'll turn toward the house, then back again,
my boots making a full circle in the snow.
A gray squirrel will jump onto the pyre,
eyes staring up into my bloodshot eyes,
head tilted at an odd angle,
curious about what I might do next.

Midnight Attempts to Keep Me Calm

Lois Roma-Deeley

I close my eyes,
imagine a white field of new snow.
The sun, a pearl disk, fills my mind.
A thousand cranes hang from an alabaster sky.
Suddenly, bitter winds kick up.
Icicle bones drop beside dead trees,
cracking the heart of this scene. I'm drifting
but can't sleep.

Solstice

Ed Ruzicka

Originally published in My Life in Cars *by Ed Ruzicka (2020)*

Wheat weighted with snow.
Bone moon working like a bleach.
Corn stubble, stark, vast.

To the Man Who Can't Tell Me He Loves Me

Claire Marsden

To the man who can't tell me he loves me
because of his faith—
I thought I was a feminist
but look at me,
you've put me in a chrysalis
and I'm turning into sludge.

It's the transition that's the hardest.
The silence. The space.
The time I need to fill.
I should be angry with you. I should call you out
for being a coward.
But who can harbor malice for a man,
such a sweet, sweet man
who uses words like muddle?

11:02 to 11:27—Shower.
Washed hair and body.
Thought of you for twenty-four minutes.
One minute less than yesterday.

There's a pine tree outside the window.
Evergreen.
I admire its tenacity
and give quiet thanks.

Winter

Claire Marsden

They tell me it's transitory,
this deep cut.
That it will heal and scab over.
That I will, eventually, recognize
its true nature.
Do they not see?
I'm not ready to stop the bleeding.
Let the crows come and peck
at my flesh.
I do not wish to forget
you yet.

Songlines

Claire Marsden

You came across me
as I wandered in the woods,
nameless.
You sang me into existence,
and joy was mine.
But other creatures needed your voice
and you vanished,
leaving your footprints in the snow.

The Song
in the Well

Rebecca Harrison

There is no music now. Not on Sundays, when the bells used to clamor clear and fill the valley right to the top like cream poured onto porridge, and Gwyn used to swing my hand as we tramped between the wild poppies, our eyes on the blue hills, our noses twitching from the meadow grass. When we told time by dandelions, and the choir songs brimmed out the church, spilling up and up. That was before Pa fought for the king. Before the country changed like a wood changes when the trees have molted, and the leaves crushed brown and slippery.

Pa didn't come home, and his chair stayed by the fire, the one I sat by, resting against the side, my eyes slits just open enough to let in a bit of the fire glow, my face turned red as an apple polished on a sleeve. Pa used to sing in his evening voice, the one different to his Sunday voice kept for choir that was as shining as the saints' halos. This voice was a long whisper, like the gloaming in our window.

After Pa had gone, there was only silence. A silence marked like a footprint on snow. And I felt it mark me, too. My bones were sore with it, and I walked under the valley sky, leaden and slow.

One day, I heard Pa's evening voice, low and lilting. I tried not to hear it. The horizon was turning the color of buttercups and the geese were noisy silhouettes, and I heard the voice coming from the old well by the church. I crept near and looked down into the gloomy waters and it rang echo-y about me. And I called into the well, but my own voice vanished and there was only Pa's song, like a stream on a summer's eve. So, I lowered the bucket and scooped it up.

I carried the song home in the bucket, and it slopped about but rang pure over my path like a lantern in the dark. I put the bucket on my father's chair. And when Ma came in, we stood with our arms around each other and listened. Our smiles were all tears.

And the winter came and turned the valley to stillness and sparkle. The silence out there didn't reach us, for we had Pa's song in the bucket, and it made our small home warm, even though the windows were so thick with frost you couldn't see out, even though the firewood was meager and gave little heat. There'd been no Christmas since the king had died. No merry bit of color in the cruel cold. And I remembered Pa singing the Christmas dawn, his voice like stars growing wings. So, I took the bucket and I climbed to the top of the valley, my boots slipping on the frosted paths, my breath cold steam. I lifted the bucket high and poured out Pa's song, and it filled the valley all Christmas morn and longer into the dark.

there was only silence

my bones were sore with it

Breaking Point

Jessica Kim

I sip the hours like chamomile
tea. *This is your medicine* and mother
would brew admonitions into the
mixture: remember to wash the dishes,
it's time you stop wearing the dresses
you've outgrown. I only dream of
freedom and girlhood. I hide ribbons in
tree trunks, chiseling prayers for a magic
treehouse; take me somewhere else.

Shapeshift. Tell me *I am the moon* and
cradle me in those love-soaked palms.
Lopsided constellations dangle from
the night sky where nothing is
permanent. *Mother, can you find me
here?* In the receding valleys of my
widow's peak, early sunlight scattered
like strands of white hairs. The way my
face contours into riverbeds and I learn
what it means to age, the way a girl
tramples on bruised soil, unnoticed.

Instead, mother teaches me how to
cut the bellies of fruit without remorse,
how to forget her existence and one day
she will be gone. *Be strong, girl.*
Tonight, the blood-thirsty crescent feeds
on my cartilage with a mischievous grin
and I am reminded of how the world
is still a stranger, stripping away my
childhood like pork meat, the
bleached bones rattling to the floor.

Mom's Hot Chocolate

Alexa Hailey

I thought that if my mother made it for me, it would taste like childhood. That could be the key, the time machine. It could transport me to a point before desperate loneliness, before lovers who took everything, even the cat.

My hot chocolate had failed. I sat and drank it in an empty kitchen, and it took me nowhere and brought me nothing. Mom's didn't taste like this—grainy powder, with congealed balls that exploded to dust on my tongue. Hers tasted safe, like someone who would always love me. And it tasted like milk. Not watery at all.

So I went home. It was that easy. My mom still lived in the same house, as she often reminded me in the long-winded voicemails she left, the ones that I barely ever listened to. She thinks I have a tape answering machine, like the one we had when I was a kid. You had to listen to the whole message before you could delete it, which was convenient for neglected mothers hoping to guilt-trip their children into a call. My voicemail is digital. I swipe her messages aside with one finger, and they're gone.

The outside of the house was a mess. Overgrown shrubs reached out of the chain-link fence to snag passersby and pull them inside. *Help us*, they screamed. *Witness this.* It wasn't a shock, I told myself. Dad took care of the yard. I'll tell her to hire someone? Is that what kids are supposed to do for their parents?

Mom didn't look much better. She answered the door in an old house dress with all sorts of colorful stains down the front. This thing had seen multiple meals. She said, "Oh, it's you," and I said, "I need some of your hot chocolate," and she nodded and turned into the house. Her hair had a knot at the back that was bigger than my fist.

Inside things were much worse. I followed Mom through a maze of piled magazines, scraps of cloth, and boxes that boasted "As Seen on TV!" A metal hanger caught my belt loop in the hallway. Before I could untangle myself, it whispered *You're here now. You can't unsee this.* I shoved it back further into the mountain of trash.

Mom chatted to me as we wandered through the labyrinth, updating me on this friend, that cousin, and that thing she saw on the news. "Could that be true?" she asked.

I opened my mouth and my heart jumped out. It flopped hopelessly on top of an old box of Depends that were left over from when Dad was sick. "Yeah, maybe," I croaked.

I sat in silence as Mom put the water on the stove and rummaged around in cabinets and piles, eventually pulling out a can of Swiss Miss. I told myself I'd watch how she made it so I could do it myself at home, in my cozy apartment in the city, away from this crap town. But I found myself focusing on a piece of paper that stuck out from a pile next to the back burner. It danced closer and closer to the flame, until eventually flames flew around the bottom of the pot.

"Mom! Fire!"

She turned casually, shut off the stove, and batted at the fire with her fingers until the flames were gone.

"Oh, that happens sometimes." She smiled sheepishly.

I looked around the kitchen. Grease stained the back of the stove. Was that mold on the dishes? The drawings I'd given her as a child were still taped to the cabinet fronts. They were yellow and faded but still there.

I was already locking them away, preparing a corner of my mind where this afternoon would go. I would put all the old lovers there too, and the cat. It would be as hidden as my father's ashes, sitting somewhere under all this rubble. I could forget the house, forget the fire, and keep only the flavor of the hot chocolate.

Mom put the cup down in front of me. It was the perfect temperature, as always. I closed my eyes and took a long, deep sip. It tasted just the same. The milk, sugar, and cocoa were perfectly blended, seamless. In that moment, nothing mattered. It worked. In that moment, I was a child again. And in the next, I was gone. I drove away from the house, back to desperate loneliness, back to a clean apartment with lumpy hot chocolate and no cat. As for my mother, I had already forgotten her again, even though the taste of her hot chocolate still lingered on my tongue.

Persolus, Patron Saint of Isolation

Paulie Lipman

Look upon me
shallow eyed
and know
that we both
bear witness
and embrace a
gentle sadness at
life's impermanence

When Sadness
gives way to Fear
when you feel like
you can't leave, that
this forlorn congregation
is of your own construction
that you as both host
and only guest must
keep going
the difference
between

peace
　　　and seclusion

is never
　　　　clearer

With
              solitude
                  comes
reflection
         which
             leads
      to
clarity

In
                    isolation
comes realization
remembrance that
that we exist
                   outside
of our own perception
that we are formed by
and made of many
across this expanse
right down to the blood
and that distance will
never break this
synthesis

we exist

                                        outside

of our own perception

Medius, Patron Saint of Uncertainty

Paulie Lipman

Originally published in Unlikely Stories Mark V *(October 2020)*

I'm sorry
I can't be
as honest
as your face
chin down
mouth fraught
eyes that won't
let the light in

and I strangely
have no words

In this time
as in every
we are all
terrified
only begotten
children locked
in the same room
all our hurt
lying atop
each other's
simply
drawing breath
with no perception
how the next
may come

I, as you
am afflicted
with this doubt
and only able
to offer up the
palest of shelter
thin and unsure
built from a notion
ancient but rendered
bizarre from misuse:

That whatever
will alleviate this
must be built
and learned from
each other, but
more than anything
we must never
allow it to be
unkind
That is
the only thing
we can ever
be sure of

and I strangely

have no words

Steven without the T

Lew Furber

"You look repulsive when you cry" is an eight-syllable sentence that caused me to stay silent for eight days and therefore lose my job, but that didn't matter to Janice. I could tell she had tried to improve her appearance that day because she had set her hair solid with something that smelled like vodka. I always laughed when she had sprayed her hair because she usually made herself look like a pharaoh.

When Janice cried she showed almost all of her teeth, like a baboon. I don't think anyone wants to look ugly when they have tried to be pretty, so I said what I said because I thought she had forgotten she had tried to look nice. I should have said, "Why are you crying, Janice? Is it because you are fat?" This would have been much better because it is conversational, rather than a statement, and she has cried about being fat in the past. It would have shown I have been listening. It is also two seven-syllable sentences.

Nine days later I sat in the quiet carriage on the train to Nottingham. I had been allowed to speak for twenty-six hours, but I am always alone on Sundays and never speak anyway. I groaned and held it for forty-nine seconds. This was a new record for me. I have always run out of breath at forty-two.

A lady in the seat next to me asked if I was okay.

"I am absolutely fine," I said in a voice like scrunching tissue paper.

The lady made her mouth and eyebrows point downward. People do this when they are concerned.

I said, "Memento mori, lady" to make her feel better.

The lady moved to a different seat. People often move away from me, but that's okay. I like having more room.

Mum picked me up from the station in the bad car. The bad car had a big engine that vibrated down my ears and made my brain scream.

"Hi Mum, where is the good car?"

"This is a perfectly good car, Steven, and you'll have to get used to it. We gave the other one to Janice." It sounded like Mum was snipping the ends off her words. Her mouth and eyebrows were pointing downward like the lady on the train. She might have been upset about the fourteen voicemails she had left me that week, but I didn't ask her about it.

"Janice has the good car now? Why didn't she pick me up?"

"I wonder why," Mum said, but she wasn't wondering. She often told lies like this. She put the car into third gear, and the engine started to make the bad noise. I put my fingers in my ears.

"How could you say something so hurtful to her on such a day?" She was referring to when I called Janice ugly at her husband's funeral. She had mentioned it in her voicemails.

"I know what I should have said: 'Why are you crying, Janice? Is it because you are fat?'"

"No, you absolutely should not have said that, Steven."

"But it's conversational."

"No, it isn't. You should have said, 'I'm sorry for your loss, Janice. I'm here for you if you need me.'" Mum was shouting, so I pressed my fingers further into my ears.

"But they're both eight syllables," I said.

She pulled the car in front of a Greggs.

"Why are you stopping here, Mum? I thought we were having dinner with Peter and Linda."

"And how many syllables was that, Steven?"

"They were seven and fourteen."

"You will apologize to your sister. You will say all the things you should have said. Today will be hard enough."

We were going to celebrate Janice's husband's birthday with his parents in Nottingham, even though he died. Mum said everyone would be sad, so I should wear a tie. I'm not sure why I should wear a tie because people are sad, so I brought a packet of tissues.

Peter and Linda's house was bigger than Mum's, and it had many small tables you couldn't use because they had flowers and figurines and photo frames on them. There was a room you weren't allowed to go in, even if you were Peter.

Everyone was standing in the living room with their shoes on when I arrived, except Janice, who was sitting down with her shoes on.

"I'm very sorry, Janice. I am always here for you," I said. I'm not sure what that meant, as I am rarely at Peter and Linda's house, but Janice seemed to enjoy what I said because she smiled at me.

"I know you are," she said. She hugged me, and I could smell the vodka spray in her hair.

"You look quite like a pharaoh," I said, and she made a noise like a laugh.

We sat around the table in the forbidden room. Linda had roasted a chicken for us, but we weren't allowed to eat it yet because Peter was talking.

"Today would have been Eric's thirty-sixth birthday," he said.

"He still is thirty-six, though. He's just dead now, isn't he?" I said.

Mum smacked my thigh with the back of her hand. "Be

quiet. Don't interrupt," she said.

Linda and Janice were looking down at their laps. They must have been texting because Peter is boring.

"Eric is not here anymore, Steven. You're right. But we will not forget him. We will always make room for him," said Peter. He gestured toward an empty chair, in front of which Linda had put plates and cutlery. Everyone kept glancing at the chair and sniffing and sometimes letting little tears come out. I took the packet of tissues out of my pocket and put it on the chair. Linda made a noise like she had accidentally swallowed a ping-pong ball.

"Steven, for Christ's sake. What are you doing?" Mum was hissing but she was also crying.

"Everyone keeps looking at the chair and crying, so I put the tissues on it. Now you all know where they are."

"Apologize to Peter and Linda."

"I can't do that because there are too many syllables."

"Ridiculous," said Peter.

"You will apologize. You are not helping. Be respectful," said Mum.

I thought I had been helpful. Mum didn't agree and she had shown it by shouting at me in the car and later at the dinner table. She was always upset when I talked about the syllables. She hasn't let me talk about them since the time I had to read some Shakespeare aloud at school and didn't speak for the rest of the term. She used to say I have a rich inner life, but she doesn't say that anymore.

"I have a rich inner life," I said. I saw Linda counting to seven on her fingers.

"Shut up, Steven," said Mum.

Linda allowed us to eat the chicken after Peter had stopped talking about Eric's birthday. It was very moist, which I hoped was not because she had cried on it. Janice was telling a story about Eric. Everyone laughed at it, but they didn't say anything else for four seconds afterward. It was Peter who spoke first.

"How's work, Steven?"

"It's fine, but I got fired."

"What? Why?" said Janice.

Mum threw her cutlery on her plate and sat back. Maybe she could taste the tears, too.

"I had to do a silence."

Mum whispered something I couldn't hear, but it was probably "For fuck's sake."

"That's terrible," said Peter. "But how are you getting on *otherwise?*"

Peter always asked me this so I had prepared an answer on the train: "I am a tired donkey, fruitlessly mashing the keys of the ATM of life. Memento mori, Steven. You'll be with Eric soon. He's had all of his problems. He won't have more now he's dead. Sometimes I wish I was dead. This is the longest I've ever spoken out loud, you know."

Nobody replied to me, but Janice started crying.

"Why are you crying, Janice?" I said. "Is it because you are fat?"

Peter stood up and told me to get out of his house.

"'Tired' only has one syllable," said Linda.

"It does in your posh accent," I said.

"I agree with Linda," said Mum.

"Get out, Steven," said Peter.

"I don't know why you're upset," I said.

Linda counted to seven on her fingers and said, "Fuck it."

Mum took me to the door. "When will this end, Steven? You couldn't be nice for one fucking day." I knew she didn't mean "nice." She meant "normal."

"I thought I was being nice. I even bought a present. Eric doesn't live here now, so I had it delivered to the graveyard where he is."

She closed the door, and it made a loud banging sound that made my brain scream.

I had upset them somehow. It stung me a little that they rejected my tissue idea. I thought it would make Peter happy to know it was still Eric's thirty-sixth birthday because then it wouldn't be pointless to celebrate it. I don't know why Mum was angry all day, especially about sending Eric's gift to the graveyard. I sent him flowers. I thought dead people liked flowers.

People often don't want to hear an apology straight away. Janice told me that, and I think she was right. People seem to accept apologies if they come with gifts, though, so I started to walk to the shops.

Eric and I had walked from his parents' house to the shops many times. Janice never came with us. The last time we went, Eric took me to the board game café and he played Risk with me for three hours. The café closed before our game ended, and Eric took me to the pub and bought me a pint of beer. No one had taken me to the pub and bought me a pint of beer before. Not on my own, anyway.

My eyes felt wet and dry at the same time. I stopped by a shop whose windows were covered in stickers about the cost of phoning someone in Bangladesh. I went inside because I had taken a wrong turn while I was thinking about Eric and I had lost my way. I asked the shopkeeper for directions.

A little scowl happened around his eyes and mouth, but he quickly hid it. People do this often when they speak to me. Janice told me it could be because I point my eyebrows downward when I talk to someone I don't know well, but I only do that because I'm concentrating. Maybe the shopkeeper scowled because he hadn't sold many phone cards for Bangladesh. I stopped pointing my eyebrows down and bought one. It didn't seem to cheer him up because he scowled and hid it again.

It is very hard to know why people say and do things. Sometimes it seems like everybody else has access to a script because they always seem to know what should happen next. When I was seven, I was off school for two weeks with the flu, so maybe they gave everyone the script then. I usually try not to think about it. It makes me so upset I become sleepy.

I used to work in an office where people scowled and hid it from me. I never asked why they were lying about their feelings to me because they might have said something upsetting. My manager scowled the most. She hid many scowls during a meeting about what work people call "reasonable adjustments." I told her I needed some changes at work to stop my brain screaming. She agreed to change some things, but she never did.

She didn't bother to hide her scowls in our next meeting when I asked her why she hadn't made the changes yet. I guess I had said something that wasn't in the script. I quit that job because I didn't want my brain to scream anymore. Mum was angry about that. Everyone pretends they will make room for people who are different, but they get tired of pretending when they actually have to do something.

I arrived at the shops while I was thinking. I went to John Lewis because Peter and Linda had lots of John Lewis carrier bags in their bag of carrier bags under the sink. I took an expensive photo frame to the till because there were no cheap ones.

"This is because Eric died," I said.

"I'm sorry?" said the lady at the till.

"Apology accepted."

"What?"

"Where can I print some photos?"

She told me to go to the supermarket, and I used the machine in there to print a picture from my phone. It was a picture I had taken of Eric last year. He was standing outside and smiling, and he was holding a toy Gandalf I had seen in a shop and bought for him. I had the same photo in my living room.

It had been nearly two hours since Peter and Mum had shouted at me. This was enough time for them to calm down and eat their teary chicken. When Janice let me in the front door, she patted me on my shoulder, but she didn't smile.

She took me to the living room, where everyone had finally taken off their shoes. The TV was on, but it looked like everyone had been glaring at the doorway waiting for me to come in.

"What do you have to say for yourself, then?" Mum said. She was sitting in an armchair facing away from me, so she had to turn her neck all the way around like an owl.

"It's for Peter and Linda," I said.

I saw Linda counting on her fingers and mouthing my words silently.

"What? What is?"

I took the frame out of the carrier bag and gave it to Peter, who had been keeping his face very still. "I got the bag you like, too. I'll put it under the sink."

"Wait," said Peter. "When was this taken? I haven't seen it before."

"Me neither," said Linda, which made Janice look at it too. Two tears fell out of Linda's eyes.

"Is it not a good picture?" I said.

Nobody said anything, so after seven seconds I sat down. Peter and Linda passed the photo frame to Janice, who looked at it but still didn't speak. She held the frame in her lap, and after a while she made a comment about the TV to Linda.

Everyone looked at the TV, but I don't think they were watching it. I thought I should say something, even though no one had said thank you. "I'm sorry I upset you," I said to Peter, then Linda, then Janice, then Mum.

Nobody replied. They kept looking at the TV.

Snow for Your Birthday

E. Samples

January 4, 2017

I don't have to get you anything this year,
but I wonder if there's anything you need.

January moons will come blue and go
whether river water flows or freezes,
whether coal skips, sinks, or smolders
heaped on the sandbar.

This birthday crunches under boots barely leaving prints.
Fresh cold falls,
sharp and white.
My palm holds pieces for my mind to trace
from one unfixed point to the next
over ridge and hollow.

What ungiven gift says it best?
Like you, these lines will always be unfinished.

December, Outside Exit 110

E. Samples

And were I to go back, up the stairs to the old hall,
Past the third step, cracking ice,
The tenth, its warped dark board,
Turn the corner at the gold framed mirror—
Who will greet me at each door:
A young self,
A ghost self,
A relative?
And were I a witness, pattern in the ivy frosted wall,
Quiet mist rolling over interred summer green,
Settling like snow against steadfast brick,
The millstone grinds to the skeleton swing—
What book will reveal its truth to me:
The watercolor tale,
The remastered dream,
The creased *In Loving Memory*?

rivulet

E. Samples

train ride through a town
before
my arrival
before
you find out about me
before we live in
its old house its
winding farm road
breathe its sweet
hanging tobacco
before
your last words
before
you die on its couch

traveling   speeds of light, key changes
through   foggy pike, terminal trees

after the night's
broken threshold
after
its metallic slam
after
its black plastic body bag
after we stand behind
its kitchen counter
numb-stained watching
you roll out

---

after
your last text
after
words remain

Tears of joy.
Just tears of joy.[*]

[*] The final text I received from my dad before he died.

before
your last words

Orange Ribbon for Multiple Sclerosis

Morgan Russell

My mother—
the Diminutive Canyon,
not a thousandth world wonder,
but a sight to see.

Haunted houses
are no match
for haunted hollows
where skin gnaws bone.

Concave where I wish for convex.
Limbs tucked close
atrophic from disuse.
Life sucks the marrow from bone.

Not a death sentence;
I recall the doctor's words.
I watch her fade to nothing
stuck in her bed and I know
prolonged
suffering
is much worse than death.

Burnout

Kendra Nuttall

My childhood bathroom had brown carpet,
twenty years of stains embedded in the fibers
under my bare feet. It didn't bother me then.
Tonight, I'm lying awake on a motel mattress,
searching for stars hidden somewhere
beyond the city lights.
I haven't seen them in years.
How many people have slept in these sheets?
How many hands have touched these towels?
How many feet have walked across this carpet?
You could vacuum and scrub and never erase
all the memories and skeletons and dirt
trapped inside these four walls.
We tore out the bathroom carpet
when it came time to sell the house,
but there's no hiding behind a remodel.
Every home has its secrets.
Every star burns out.

Christmas Eve

Kendra Nuttall

I'm sitting in front of the muted TV
watching images flash across the screen—
Channel 2 News making poinsettia bouquets,
Clark Griswold carving the Christmas turkey,
lips moving in frenetic silence.
I'm listening for the hum of my father's snores
to know that he's still breathing.
To know that he's still alive.
It's always winter here.
This house never catches the sun in time.
My father's frail body is unrecognizable
under a flurry of fleece, his face
the color of day-old snow. To think,
he was the man who sang at my wedding
only three months ago. It was winter then too,
we just didn't see the frost written in the lawn.
We never do, until no blanket can
capture the warmth we crave.

Good and Valuable Consideration

Frances Boyle

Winter is a contract, made between cloudless
sky and the frozen earth, an emissary of snow
blustering between them.
                            Winter is an exhale
as long as a kite tail, wandering and wavering
in the open field.
                        Last winter was a slope
of ice I could try to grip but inevitably
slid along, instants of pure gliding grace
followed by flailing for balance, windmill
arms and stutter-step feet.
                            Winter is never
as long as you remember, or as short
as in flickering celluloid, the blur
when sprockets slip, strip. Winter

        is emotion trapped behind
a steady blue gaze, imperious
and unforgiving. Ah, but winter is

icy air   lungs purified
by bounteous exertion   moving skis
along tracks   the openness of sky,
its dove-gray   the evergreens
near black but garlanded with white-blue

—winter's currency, its fee for service.

Dear Winter

Kaci Skiles Laws

It's the first Christmas since my sister passed.
I want to tell you she died peacefully and how—
my family is not a Hallmark card,

this is supposed to be
a happy time.

I forget she is gone some days, think of
things to say for a millisecond.
I remember I can't, not out loud, maybe,
as a whisper to you.

I confess; I call her.
I hit send and receive

white noise. She can never answer.
Dad said he'd keep the line
until the end of the year.

I hesitate to leave messages at the beep,
like a tree adjusting to the sudden drop
and envelope of arctic air,
at the sound of her voice.

I hang up. I howl like the wind after it
holds its breath, exhales—*cold is here,*

collects like dust on the forest's
hibernating eyelids.

I can't speak. I write letters. I tie them.
I add in all the old tatters I don't want,

that were returned to me
to keep. I imagine her hands
tearing into them.

I keep her pages. I'm gifting you the rest,
what's left of this season. I watch them, wait

to be seen
from beneath my window's buckling knees.
I hope a bird might find them
and make a bed, maybe, a nest
for new life.

I'm gifting you the rest, what's left of this season

Alpha and Omega

Kathryn Sadakierski

Pink-skied winter,
In its first blush
Is like rosy-cheeked children coming inside after sledding,
After winter breathed its life into their bones.
The sky's brilliant paint colors
Almost compensate for the light's early departure;
Under gauzy veils of snow, the world quiets,
In awe.

The trees, scraggly
As worn-out paint brushes,
Muffle the landscape in a raspy cough
Blurred across the plains.
Alone, in the barren fields,
The grass blades weep,
Frosty tears left like commas
Mid-sentence, in their fingers,
As they brush away memories
Of summer, before they were frozen,
Paused.

So winter begins the season
And it ends,
Refreshing the land
Before it starts again,
Born into new flowers and rushing rivers
Coursing through the veins of ravines
Like young blood.
What is old finds new life,
As winter extends its bony hand
For us to take,
And the sun sets faster
Than in days past.

Waning Refrain

Kathryn Sadakierski

I watch quietly as the sun slips in silver quarters
Down the mountainside,
Blinding me briefly before it blinks its eye.
The rancorous din of the coldness that follows
Is sunset's only twin, and only I am privy to it.
As the bird sings its diamond-throated trills
That give me chills,
The world sits, breathlessly holding still.

Seen in a small niche upon the hill
In its tender folds, partly obfuscated by shrubs,
The front window of the farmhouse that faces the sun
Resembles a bleary-eyed badger
Emerging from the frost-encrusted ground
To blink at the dawn
As a pale sheen of light trickles like water
In a reflection on the precipice of night.

There's a sharpness about the land's hunger
That makes you more alert,
Like the pang sadness gives you,
Heartache
Reminding you not to get hurt.
The wheat fields have frozen
Under the silent fires of winter's fury,
And the vibrant colors of the sunset
Have been swept away,
Like faded paints
Under layers of dirt,
Flowers buried below the earth
In threads sewn cold.

The bare, sown fields, lonely in the dark cold,
Glitter with frost,
The burnished strings of grass tightly huddled,
Knit further into the dirt
For warmth from winter's unsmiling earth,
Yarn woven into the hard-packed ground
That doesn't tremble with footsteps
Making imprints on the clay.

What I wouldn't give
To have back
Summer's rosy-eyed mirth.

Contributors

Frances Boyle is the author of two poetry books, most recently *This White Nest* (Quattro Books, 2019) and *Seeking Shade*, a short story collection (The Porcupine's Quill, 2020), as well as *Tower*, a Rapunzel-inspired novella (Fish Gotta Swim Editions, 2018). She is a Canadian author living in Ottawa whose writing has recently appeared or is forthcoming in *Best Canadian Poetry 2020*, *Blackbird*, *Feral*, *Dreich*, *Event*, *Prairie Fire*, and *Parentheses Journal*. Visit francesboyle.com for more.

john compton is a thirty-three-year-old gay poet who lives in Kentucky. His poetry resides in his chest like many hearts, and they bloom like vigorously infectious wild flowers. He lives in a tiny town with his husband josh and their eight dogs and two cats. He feels his head is an auditorium filled with the dead poets from the past. He has published one book, which is being rereleased, and has six chapbooks published and forthcoming: *trainride elsewhere* (Pressed Wafer, 2016; Rogue Wolf Press, TBA), *that moan like a saxophone* (Kindle, 2016), *ampersand* (Plan B Press, 2019), *a child growing wild inside the mothering womb* (Ghost City Press, June 2020), *i saw god cooking children / paint their bones* (Blood Pudding Press, October 2020), *burning his matchstick fingers his hair went up like a wick* (Black Heart Press, March 2021), and *to wash all the pretty things off my skin* (Ethel Zine & Micro-Press, 2021). He has been published in numerous magazines and anthologies.

Savannah Cooper is a Missouri native who now lives in Maryland with her partner and dogs. Her work has previously appeared in *Mud Season Review*, *Steam Ticket*, *Gone Lawn*, *Midwestern Gothic*, and *Rust + Moth*, among other publications.

Linda M. Crate has work published in numerous magazines and anthologies both online and in print. She is the author of six poetry chapbooks, the latest of which is *More Than Bone Music* (Clare Songbirds Publishing House, 2019). She's also the author of the novel *Phoenix Tears* (Czykmate Books, 2018). Recently she has published two full-length poetry collections, *Vampire Daughter* (Dark Gatekeeper Gaming, February 2020) and *The Sweetest Blood* (Cyberwit, February 2020).

Mary Alice Dixon lives and writes in Charlotte, North Carolina, where she is a long-time hospice volunteer. She is working on a collection of poems and short fiction exploring illness, loss, and end-of-life issues. She is also a former attorney who often served as a guardian ad litem in adult incompetency cases. In addition, she has been an unsuccessful door-to-door encyclopedia seller, a successful backyard gardener, and a professor. Her recent work is in or forthcoming from *Kakalak*, *Main Street Rag*, *Stonecoast Review*, *The Mythic Circle*, *County Lines*, *That Southern Thing*, Living Springs Publishers, and elsewhere.

Nancy K. Dobson has writing, both fiction and poetry, published in a variety of journals including *The Sun*, *Noyo River Review*, *Five on the Fifth*, and *ARDOR*. Her poetry has won a few prizes. When not writing, she enjoys hiking beautiful trails or upcycling fashion.

Glennys Egan was raised in the Canadian prairies and now lives in Ottawa, Ontario, where she works for the government like everyone else. She holds a BA and an MA from Carleton University. Her poetry has been published in *Taco Bell Quarterly*. You can find her and her dog, Boris, online at @gleegz.

Shufei Ewe (she/her) is a copywriter, dreamer, cereal hoarder, and serial overthinker. Her work has been featured or is forthcoming in *Versification*, *The Adriatic Magazine*, *Yes Poetry*, and *HAD*.

Lew Furber is a neurodivergent writer in Cardiff, UK. He is also a guitarist, composer, guitar teacher, and one half of a surrealist musical comedy act, in which he wears a gray old lady wig and white face paint for little discernible reason. He has work forthcoming in a number of magazines, and in 2020 he was longlisted for the Galley Beggar Press Short Story Prize.

John Grey is an Australian poet, US resident, recently published in *Soundings East*, *The Dalhousie Review*, and *Connecticut River Review*, with work upcoming in *West Trade Review*, *Willard and Maple*, and *The MacGuffin*.

Alexa Hailey is a freelance and fiction writer from Massachusetts. Her fiction work has been published in *Spelk*, *Flash Fiction Magazine*, *Vamp Cat Magazine*, and others. Follow her on Twitter at @lexabobexa.

Rebecca Harrison sneezes like Donald Duck, and her best friend is a dog who can count.

Eddie L House (they/them) is a manic pixie dream-queer who enjoys roller-skating, mainlining caffeine, and smoking out of windows. You can find more of their work in *Anatolios*, *ImageOutWrite*, or tucked inside library books around the Stoke-on-Trent area.

Swastika Jajoo is a queer poet studying theoretical linguistics in Japan. She won the second prize in the poetry contest organized as part of the international Glass House Poetry Festival. She has been published with *Riggwelter*, *Muse India*, and *Huffington Post*, among others, and her spoken word pieces have been featured on UnErase Poetry, one of India's leading spoken word content producers. She was also invited to perform with *Rolling Stone India* for Pride Month 2020.

Jessica Kim is a writer based in California with works appearing or forthcoming in *Cosmonauts Avenue*, *Glass: A Journal of Poetry*, *Yes Poetry*, and more. Her poems have recently been recognized by the National Poetry Quarterly and Pulitzer Center. She loves all things historical and sour.

Kayla King is the author of *These Are the Women We Write About*, a micro-collection of poetry published by The Poetry Annals. She is the founding editor and contributing writer for *Pages Penned in Pandemic: A Collective*, forthcoming publication January 2021. Kayla's fiction and poetry have been published by or are forthcoming from *Fireworords Magazine*, *Sobotka Literary Magazine*, and *Honey & Lime*, among others. You can follow Kayla's writing journey over at kaylakingbooks.com or her twitterings at @KaylaMKing.

Kaci Skiles Laws is a closet cat lady and creative writer living in Dallas–Fort Worth. Her work has been featured in *The Letters Page*, *Bewildering Stories*, *The American Journal of Poetry*, *Pif Magazine*, and *The Blue Nib*, among others. Her published work and blog can be viewed at kaciskileslawswriter.wordpress.com.

Noah Letscher is a recent graduate from St. Olaf College with a BA in English and theater. They spend most of their time that they're not working at their remote job engaged in some form of creation for Dungeons & Dragons. They are in three and a half ongoing campaigns, which leaves them little time to write, but like any writer, they manage. Their favorite place to be is wherever they can light a nice-smelling candle. Noah is notoriously bad at titling anything.

Paulie Lipman is a former bartender/bouncer/record store employee/Renaissance Fair worker/two-time National Poetry Slam finalist and a current loud Jewish/queer/poet/writer/performer. His work has appeared in *Button Poetry*, *Write About Now*, *The Emerson Review*, *Drunk in a Midnight Choir*, *Voicemail Poems*, *pressure gauge*, *Protimluv* (Czech Republic), and *Prisma: Zeitblatt für Text & Sprache* (Germany). Their poetry collections *from below/denied the light* (2018) and *sad bastard soundtrack* (2019) are available from Swimming with Elephants Publications.

Kirsten Luckins is a poet, performer, and creative producer living on the northeast coast of England. Her previous two collections have been published by Burning Eye Books, and her third collection (from which this poem is taken) will be released by Bad Betty Press in February 2021. She is the artistic director of the Tees Women Poets women's performance poetry collective. She blogs at kirstenluckins.com.

Eva Lynch-Comer holds a BA in creative writing from Hamilton College, where she received the John V. A. Weaver Prize in Poetry and the Sydna Stern Weiss Essay Prize in Women's Studies. Her work has appeared in the Hamilton College publications *Grasping Roots* and *The Spectator*. She was a poetry editor of the campus literary journal *Red Weather*. Eva now works in children's editorial at a publishing company in New York City. Her hobbies include playing with her dog Osito, reading YA fantasy novels, drinking chai tea, and reading outside on her front porch where she can enjoy nature.

Isabella J Mansfield writes about the many faces of anxiety, body image, intimacy, and the human condition. Most notably, Mansfield has performed at The Oberon Theatre (Cambridge, Massachusetts), Nambucca (London, UK), and at various readings and open mics across the US. Her poems have been featured by *The Wild Word*, *Sad Girl Review*, *Liminality*, and *Capsule Stories*, as well as in publications by *East Jasmine Review*, Augie's Bookshelf, and Rebel Mountain Press. In 2017, she was a Brittany Noakes Award semifinalist. She won the 2018 Mark Ritzenhein New Author Award. Finishing Line Press published her Pushcart Prize-nominated chapbook, *The Hollows of Bone*, in 2019. She lives in Howell, Michigan, with her family.

Natalie Marino is a writer, mother, and physician. She graduated with her BA in American literature from UCLA and her MD from the University of Pittsburgh. She has work in or will soon be published by *Barren Magazine*, *LEON Literary Review*, *Literary Mama*, *Louisiana Literature*, *Mineral Lit Mag*, among others. She lives in Thousand Oaks with her husband and two daughters.

Claire Marsden enjoys writing poetry, CNF, and fiction and is thrilled many of her pieces have found wonderful homes. Although she has chronic pain she has learned to dance with the dark, and when she isn't wild swimming or tramping through the woods she can usually be found squirreled away writing.

Nick Newman studies English literature at the University of Leeds. He grew up in China and Scotland. His work has appeared in *Mineral Lit Mag*, and you can find him on Twitter at @_NickNewman.

Kendra Nuttall is a copywriter by day and poet by night. Her work has previously appeared in *Spectrum*, *Capsule Stories*, and *Chiron Review*, among others. Her debut poetry collection, *A Statistical Study of Randomness*, is forthcoming from Finishing Line Press. Kendra lives and works in Utah with her husband and poodle. When she's not writing, you can find her hiking around Utah or watching reality TV. Find her online at kendranuttall.com.

Mallory Pearson is a writer and artist based in New York City. The twenty-three-year-old from Manassas, Virginia, focuses on creating work in the realm of painting, book arts, jewelry, and poetry. She received a BFA with a major in painting and a minor in book arts from Pratt Institute. She portrays themes of folklore, femininity, and loss and how these elements interact with the southern United States.

Lois Roma-Deeley's fourth poetry collection *The Short List of Certainties* (2017) won the Jacopone da Todi Poetry Book Prize. Her previous collections are *Rules of Hunger* (2004), *northSight* (2006), and *High Notes* (2010), which was a Paterson Poetry Prize Finalist. Her work is featured in or forthcoming from numerous anthologies and journals, nationally and internationally, including *Odes and Elegies*, *Feminine Rising: Voices of Power and Invisibility*, *Slipstream*, *Post Road*, *Bosque*, *Zone 3*, *Spillway*, *Artemis*, Glass Poetry Press's *Poets Resist* series, and many more. Roma-Deeley is the associate editor of the poetry journal *Presence*. You can find her online at loisroma-deeley.com.

Morgan Russell (she/they) is a rhetorician and poet from Atlanta. She believes in vulnerability first and foremost. She is the creative writing editor of *Marías at Sampaguitas*, and most of her pieces can be found at linktr.ee/morgankrussell.

Ed Ruzicka was raised beside creeks and cornfields not far from Chicago and now lives with his wife, Renee, and their doddering bulldog, Tucker, in Baton Rouge. Ed has published one full-length volume and recently had his second collection, *My Life in Cars*, published. Ed's poems have appeared in *Atlanta Review*, *Rattle*, and *New Millennium Writings*, as well as many other literary journals and anthologies. More at edrpoet.com.

Kathryn Sadakierski is a twenty-one-year-old graduate student whose writing has appeared in *Critical Read*, *Halfway Down the Stairs*, *NewPages Blog*, *Teachers of Vision*, *The Ekphrastic Review*, *The Voices Project*, *Visual Verse*, and elsewhere. She holds a BA from Bay Path University and is pursuing her master's degree.

E. Samples is from Appalachia and lives in Southern Indiana. Her writing has appeared in *Lucent Dreaming*, *Twist in Time*, *Black Bough Poetry*, *Abridged*, and elsewhere. She is on Twitter at @emilysamples.

Barbara Simmons grew up in Boston and now resides in San Jose, California. The two coasts inform her poetry. A graduate of Wellesley College, she received an MA in The Writing Seminars from Johns Hopkins. As a secondary school English

---

teacher, she loved working with students who inspired her to think about the many ways we communicate. Retired, she savors smaller parts of life and language, exploring words as ways to remember, envision, celebrate, mourn, and, always, to try to understand more about being and living and expressing her identity and humanity. Publications have included, among others, *The Quince, Santa Clara Review, Hartskill Review, Boston Accent, New Verse News, Soul-Lit, 300 Days of Sun, Capsule Stories Isolation Edition*, and *Perspectives* on KQED, the NPR local affiliate.

Abigail Swoboda is a poet and kindergarten teacher who lives in Philadelphia. Visit their website abigailswoboda.com or find them on Twitter at @orbigail.

Lucy Tyrrell writes poems that are primarily inspired by nature and wild landscapes, outdoor pursuits, family stories, and travel. In 2016, after sixteen years in Alaska, she traded a big mountain (Denali) for a big lake (Lake Superior). Lucy lives near Bayfield, Wisconsin. Her favorite verbs to live by are "experience" and "create." She is Bayfield's Poet Laureate for 2020–2021.

Editorial
Staff

Natasha Lioe, Founder and Publisher

Natasha Lioe graduated with a BA in narrative studies from University of Southern California. She's always had an affinity for words and stories and emotions. Her work has appeared in *Adsum Literary Magazine* and *Capsule Stories*, and she won the Edward B. Moses Creative Writing Competition in 2016. Her greatest strength is finding and focusing the pathos in an otherwise cold world, and she hopes to help humans tell their unique, compelling stories.

Carolina VonKampen, Publisher and Editor in Chief

Carolina VonKampen graduated with a BA in English and history from Concordia University, Nebraska and completed the University of Chicago's editing certificate program. She is available for hire as a freelance copyeditor and book designer. For more information on her freelance work, visit carolina vonkampen.com. Her writing has appeared in *So to Speak*'s blog, *FIVE:2:ONE*'s #thesideshow, *Moonchild Magazine*, and *Déraciné Magazine*. Her short story "Logan Paul Is Dead" was nominated by *Dream Pop Journal* for the 2018 Best of the Net. She tweets about editing at @carolinamarie_v and talks about books she's reading on Instagram at @carolinamariereads.

Submission Guidelines

Capsule Stories **is a print literary magazine** published once every season. Our first issue was published on March 1, 2019, and we accept submissions year-round.

Become published in a literary magazine run by like-minded people. We have a penchant for pretty words, an affinity to the melancholy, and an undeniably time-ful aura. We believe that stories exist in a specific moment, and that that moment is what makes those stories unique.

What we're really looking for are stories that can touch the heart. Stories that come from the heart. Stories about love, identity, the self, the world, the human condition. Stories that show what living in this world as the human you are is like.

We accept short stories, poems, and remarkably written essays. For short stories and essays, we're interested in pieces under 3000 words. You may include up to five poems in a single poetry submission, and please send only one story or essay at a time. Please send previously unpublished work only, and only submit to one category at a time. Simultaneous submissions are okay, but please let us know if your submission is accepted elsewhere. Please include a brief third-person bio with your submission, and attach your submission in a Word document (no PDFs, please!).

Find our full submission guidelines and current theme descriptions at capsulestories.com/submissions. We now accept submissions through Submittable at capsulestories.submittable.com/submit, or you can email your submission to us at submissions@capsulestories.com.

Connect with us!
capsulestories.com
@CapsuleStories on Twitter and Facebook
@CapsuleStoriesMag on Instagram